GOBLINS

ALICIA Z. KLEPEIS

Cavendish Square

New York

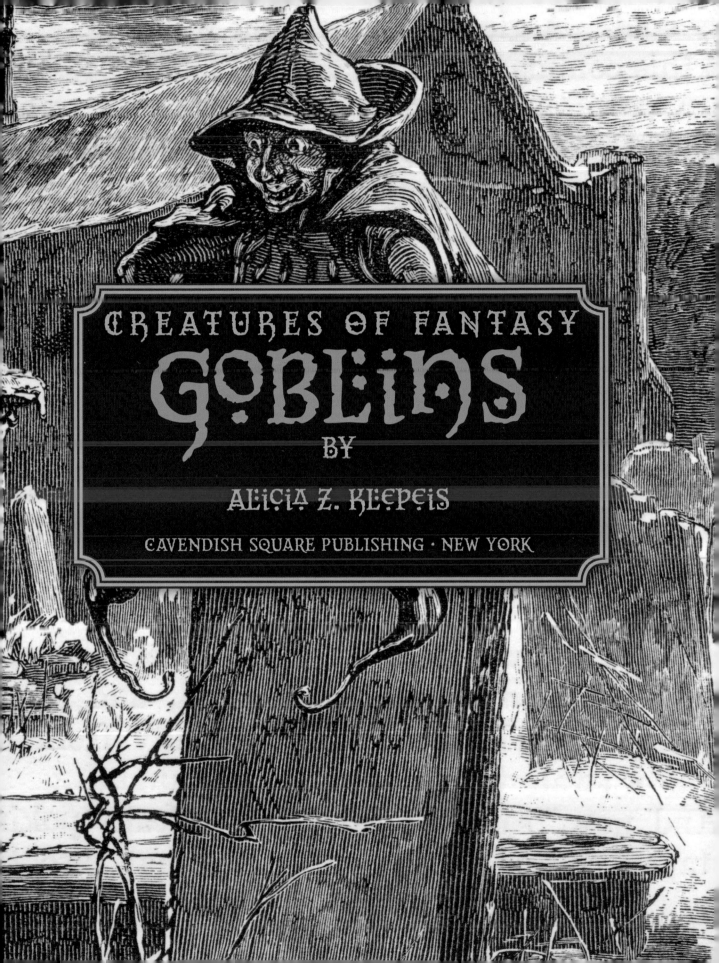

CREATURES OF FANTASY

GOBLINS

BY

ALICIA Z. KLEPEIS

CAVENDISH SQUARE PUBLISHING · NEW YORK

Published in 2016 by Cavendish Square Publishing, LLC
243 5th Avenue, Suite 136, New York, NY 10016

Copyright © 2016 by Cavendish Square Publishing, LLC
First Edition

Website: cavendishsq.com

This publication represents the opinions and views of the author based on his or her personal experience, knowledge, and research. The information in this book serves as a general guide only. The author and publisher have used their best efforts in preparing this book and disclaim liability rising directly or indirectly from the use and application of this book.

CPSIA Compliance Information: Batch #CW16CSQ

All websites were available and accurate when this book was sent to press.

Library of Congress Cataloging-in-Publication Data

Klepeis, Alicia, 1971- author.
Goblins / Alicia Z. Klepeis.
pages cm. — (Creatures of fantasy)
Includes bibliographical references and index.
ISBN 978-1-5026-0934-2 (hardcover) ISBN 978-1-5026-0935-9 (ebook)
I. Goblins—Juvenile literature. I. Title.
GR549.K63 2016
398.21—dc23
2015022183

Editorial Director: David McNamara
Editor: Kristen Susienka
Copy Editor: Nathan Heidelberger
Art Director: Jeffrey Talbot
Designer: Joseph Macri
Senior Production Manager: Jennifer Ryder-Talbot
Production Editor: Renni Johnson
Photo Research: J8 Media

Printed in the United States of America

CONTENTS

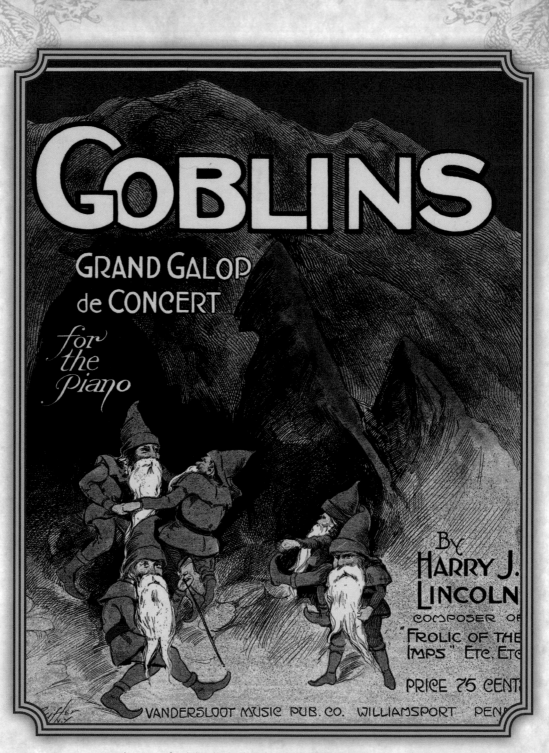

A group of goblins is depicted on the 1915 sheet music cover
for composer Harry J. Lincoln's work titled *Goblins*.

INTRODUCTION

Since the first humans walked the earth, myths and legends have engaged minds and inspired imaginations. Ancient civilizations used stories to explain phenomena in the world around them: the weather, tides, and natural disasters. As different cultures evolved, so too did their stories. From their traditions and observations emerged creatures with powerful abilities, mythical intrigue, and their own origins. Sometimes, different cultures encouraged various manifestations of the same creature. At other times, these creatures and cultures morphed into entirely new beings with greater powers than their predecessors.

Today, societies still celebrate the folklore of their ancestors—on-screen in presentations such as *The Hobbit*, *The Walking Dead*, and *X-Men*; and in stories such as *Harry Potter* and *Twilight*. Some even believe these creatures truly existed and continue to walk the earth as living creatures. Others resign these beings to myth.

In the Creatures of Fantasy series, we celebrate **captivating** stories of the past from all around the world. Each book focuses on creatures both familiar and unknown: the terrifying ghost, the bloodthirsty vampire, the classic Frankenstein, mischievous goblins, enchanting witches, and the callous zombie. Here their various incarnations throughout history are brought to life. All have their own origins, their own legends, and their own influences on the imagination today. Each story adds a new perspective to the human experience and encourages people to revisit tales of the past in order to understand their presence in the modern age.

THE ULTIMATE PRANKSTER

"They generally reward good people and punish the bad,
but being goblins they can't always be trusted."

MARTIN ROBINSON, *SEOUL*

WHETHER MISCHIEVOUS MERRY-MAKERS or violent evildoers, goblins appear differently throughout history and from one culture to another. These creatures of fantasy have captured people's imaginations for many centuries. You may have read about goblins in the pages of a Harry Potter book or spied one in a deck of Magic cards while playing with friends. From ancient folktales to modern-day films, goblins have been described in a wide variety of ways.

The Goblin Family

The goblin belongs to the fairy family, which includes creatures such as shape-shifting pookas, giant trolls, and mine-dwelling knockers.

Opposite: Three hobgoblins are enjoying beverages. Each has a different appearance, as seen in the huge hand of the center creature.

As times have changed, so has a goblin's imagery and even some of its behaviors. For example, a type of goblin known as a gremlin first appeared during the twentieth century. Later, it became forever remembered in a horror movie called *Gremlins* (1984). This new goblin specialized in messing with machinery. Since then, other goblins have also been immortalized on screens big and small.

Do these mystical creatures have anything in common? Absolutely. No matter which variety of goblin is being described, they all love making mischief and playing pranks on humankind. Some members of this chaos-causing crew steal food and clothing. Others kidnap babies. Goblins seem to revel in bringing bad luck to people around the globe. Goblins also commonly punish wicked folks who tell lies or commit crimes, or people who are lazy or greedy. However, every now and then a goblin has been known to show kindness.

Goblins are known for being fickle—that is, they are not always consistent in their behavior. A relatively kind goblin, if sufficiently irritated, will think nothing of putting a curse on a human. On the other hand, a normally evil goblin has been known to lend a hand to someone needing help.

Appearance of Goblins

While scholars often describe goblins as evil fairies, these creatures come in many forms. They range from relatively harmless hobgoblins to more violent, truly nasty creatures, including J. R. R. Tolkien's goblin-like orcs. Many people today get their perceptions of goblins from nineteenth-century legends and folktales. So what *do* goblins look like? They are typically humanlike in appearance, but many myths show them to be deformed or hideous. Goblins

Artist Hablot Knight Browne's illustration for Charles Dickens's novel *The Pickwick Papers* features a goblin sitting on an upright tombstone.

are rarely taller than 3 or 4 feet (0.9 or 1.2 meters). Their faces are horrid to look at, and their eyes are often red. It's common for a goblin to have some bizarre or unusual features, like webbed feet or pointed ears. However, some writers have taken liberty with this image. For instance, the goblins in Christina Rossetti's famous Victorian poem "Goblin Market" look more like animals:

> One had a cat's face,
> One whisked a tail,
> One tramped at a rat's pace,
> One crawled like a snail,
> One like a wombat prowled obtuse and furry,
> One like a **ratel** tumbled hurry skurry.

While it's unusual to read about or find images of female goblins in folklore, male goblins can be attired in different ways. Renowned Danish storyteller Hans Christian Andersen describes one in his story "The Elf Mound": "There came the venerable goblin chief from the Dovrefjeld, crowned with sparkling icicles and polished fir cones, muffled in his bearskin coat, and wearing his sledge-boots." A goblin in the Charles Dickens story "The Story of the Goblins Who Stole a Sexton" is described as wearing a short cloak, pointy shoes, and "a broad-rimmed sugar-loaf hat, garnished with a single feather."

Where Goblins Live

Goblins make their homes both indoors and out. They like to live in dark places. Popular outdoor locations for goblins to live include in and under the roots of old trees (especially oak trees), in mossy holes, and under rock piles. In stories as diverse as J. R. R. Tolkien's *The Hobbit* and George MacDonald's *The Princess and the Goblin*, they dwell underground in a **labyrinth** of tunnels. The type of goblin known as a bogey gets its name from living in muddy, swampy places called bogs. Legends also tell of goblins living in and around old castles and ruins, often in Europe. No matter where they choose to live, goblins can be hard to find since they tend to move around frequently.

A goblin offers scissors to a customer in "Goblin Market." She can pay for her purchase with a curl of hair.

Trading Tricksters

In fables, goblins are often depicted as merchants. Around the globe, they can be seen holding fairs or markets, offering their wares to passers-by. Italian artwork sometimes portrays red-cap goblins with weights and scales, acting like merchants. Despite the fact that goblins are members of the fairy community, they also act as traders amidst humans. This is definitely the case in "Goblin Market," where young girls Lizzie and Laura are offered the chance to buy goblin goods in the charming setting of a mossy glen. A favorite object for sale is goblin fruit, as seen in the opening lines from "Goblin Market":

Morning and evening
Maids heard the goblins cry
"Come buy our orchard fruits …
Apples and quinces,
Lemons and oranges …
Come buy, come buy"

More modern portrayals of goblins tend to be less lovely and charming than those of earlier folktales and poems. However, craftiness and the desire to trick humans have been at the heart of goblins' interactions with people since the earliest legends. The literary goblins featured in Dickens's "The Story of the Goblins Who Stole a Sexton" display some malicious behavior, though there is also humor in their portrayals.

For centuries, goblins have been associated with bad luck. People have blamed goblins for many of life's negative events. Goblins can be blamed for troublesome little occurrences like missing socks or larger-scale tragedies like mine cave-ins and deaths. Particularly in the days before scientific evidence could explain illness and other human afflictions, goblins provided perfect scapegoats for these troubles.

Holly sprigs and traditional foods appear in this illustration of the *kallikantzaroi*,
Greece's Christmas goblins. This goblin has goat feet.

CHRISTMAS CREEPERS

In many legends, goblins are active throughout the year. Yet some varieties are seasonal. Greece is home to mythical spirits known as *kallikantzaroi*. Except for during the twelve days of Christmas, these goblins live deep under Earth's surface. From December 25 through January 6 (Epiphany), the kallikantzaroi are said to venture out under the cover of darkness to cause mischief.

Greece's Christmas goblins sometimes sneak into a house by the chimney, or if particularly daring, they enter through the front door. Their mischievous misdeeds include tipping things over, breaking furniture, and spoiling food.

Since the nation's mountains and seas have separated the Greek people over the centuries, they've had differing visions of the kallikantzaroi's appearance. Some people think they have hairy bodies, monkeys' arms, red eyes, and cleft hooves. Others believe these goblins look like tall, dark-complexioned humans that wear iron clogs. They are said to live on a diet of snakes, frogs, and worms.

Believers in the kallikantzaroi have many ideas about how to keep these nasty goblins away. One is to have a blazing fire going in the hearth to prevent goblins from coming in via the chimney. Another ritual is dipping a wooden cross wrapped in basil into holy water and sprinkling the mixture all around the house to keep the kallikantzaroi away. On the island of Cyprus, people scatter pancakes on their roofs the night before Epiphany. Why? They think that offering something sweet to the kallikantzaroi is a nice gesture before the goblins depart—until the next Christmas season.

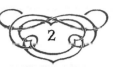

2

MINERS AND MISCHIEF MAKERS

"Goblins are cruel, wicked, and bad-hearted ... They can tunnel and mine as well as any but the most skilled dwarves, when they take the trouble, though they are usually untidy and dirty."

J. R. R. Tolkien, *The Hobbit, or There and Back Again*

FINDING OUT WHERE GOBLIN MYTHOLOGY originated is much like finding the dark, hidden-away homes of the goblins themselves—full of twists, turns, and uncertainty. Some sources say that goblin mythology originates in the Pyrenees Mountains located between France and Spain. However, from as far back as the fifth and sixth centuries CE, the people living in South Wales considered North Wales to be a land full of fairies. As author Wirt Sikes says, "In the popular imagination, that distant country was the chosen abode of giants, monsters, magicians, and all the creatures of enchantment ... Its caves and crevices have been their favorite haunt for centuries."

Opposite: Many goblins, like this one, work at Gringotts Bank in the fantasy series of Harry Potter books.

An illustration from Wirt Sikes's nineteenth-century book on British goblins shows a man dancing with fairies after entering a fairy ring.

WELSH GOBLIN MYTHOLOGY

An important figure in early goblin myths was Gwyn ap Nudd. In Welsh tradition, Gwyn ap Nudd was originally a mythological king. After the sixteenth century, he was known for being the sovereign over the fairies and the ruler over the whole goblin tribe. Ancient Welsh poetry often makes reference to Gwyn ap Nudd. His name is associated with the Vale of Neath, a scenic valley in southwestern Wales. Besides its natural wonders, this area was believed to be full of goblins that haunted people. With the dawn of the industrial age, the Vale of Neath also was home to silica mines, a prime location for underground-dwelling goblins.

An *ellylldan* is another popular goblin from Wales. It is sometimes referred to as a pooka or puck. Originally the term puck was applied to all English fairies. As expert Carol Rose writes, "He [Puck] is variously described as being a hobgoblin, a fairy, a brownie, an elf, or a goblin … He appears in numerous stories and works of literature from the earliest times, the most famous perhaps being Shakespeare's *A Midsummer Night's Dream*." William Shakespeare was very interested in Welsh folklore. Some scholars claim that Puck Valley, or Cwm Pwca, is the original setting for his sixteenth-century play *A Midsummer Night's Dream*. In the days before ironworks were established, this wooded area was said to be full of goblins.

Throughout Welsh folklore, a common tale features a goblin leading a male peasant astray. In it, the peasant returns home after a long day's work or after coming back from a fair when he notices a light moving in front of him. Taking a closer look, the person believes it is a small figure carrying a lantern or candle

above its head. The curious human follows the goblin for miles before discovering he's at the edge of a terrifying cliff. Below him he hears the sound of rushing water. Suddenly, the goblin springs over the water, landing on the other side. The evil goblin blows out its candle and leaves the peasant to find his way home in the dark.

Goblins in the Mines

Goblin mythology is rich with tales of mine-dwelling creatures. Mine-dwelling goblins go by different names depending on their location. The *coblynau* are goblins said to inhabit mining areas in Wales. They dress in mining attire; carry tiny tools such as picks, hammers, and lamps; and stand about 18 inches (45.7 centimeters) tall. Tales **abound** about the cobylnau, such as the following story about Egbert Williams, a schoolboy from Denbighshire, who was playing in a field with three girls when they observed the goblins:

> They were clothed in red like British soldiers, and wore red handkerchiefs spotted with yellow wound round their heads ... As Egbert Williams was helping his sister over they saw the coblyn close upon them, and barely got over when his hairy hand was laid on the stile. He stood leaning on it ... with a grim copper-coloured **countenance** and a fierce look.

In Cornwall, England, mine-dwelling goblins are known as knockers. These goblins are said to make knocking or thumping noises to alert human miners to where deposits of ore can be found. They also make noise to tell miners of an impending cave-in. Generally speaking, the coblynau are considered good-humored.

In exchange for their help, these goblins expect the miners to leave them food. If the humans don't fulfill their end of the deal, knockers may cause bad luck. In heavily mined **Celtic** areas, belief in these goblins used to be widespread.

The *haus-schmiedlein* were the **Bohemian** version of knockers. While it was quite rare for someone to glimpse one of these goblins, they were described as short, thickset old men with large heads. They were said to dress in the same kind of clothes as human miners. If a rich vein of silver ore was close by, the haus-schmiedlein would rap from inside the tunnel walls to let the miners know about it. The nearer the miners got to the vein, the louder the goblins would bang. If miners heard hammering from all directions, this indicated that a roof-fall was imminent and they should get out of the mine.

German folklore had its own variety of knockers called *kobolds*. These mythical creatures are thought to have come from ancient **pagan** customs. Most images depict Germany's kobolds as small, humanlike figures that dress like peasants. While some kobolds were said to reside in mines, others were just friendly household goblins that might help with chores. If these spirits felt insulted or neglected, they were likely to play tricks on their homeowners. There was also a variation on the kobold known as the *klaubautermann* that lived on ships, traveling with sailors on the open seas.

Scandinavian Goblin Lore

At first glance, it may appear that goblin folktales came only from Wales and Germany. However, other legends about goblins also abounded. Over many centuries, Scandinavian folklore told tales of goblins, dwarves, elves, and other mythical creatures. These stories are set in Midgard, the region encircled by the sea where humans lived—basically, what we call Earth today. Goblins were considered enemies of the gods. In one classic Viking tale, the chief god Odin gives the beautiful but vain goddess Freya the difficult job of commanding the weather and seasons. One day, as Freya is walking in Midgard, she comes across a cave. Since it's raining and she doesn't want to mess up her hair, she goes inside. Inside she hears noises that sound like hammers beating against the cave walls. Rounding a bend, she discovers that goblins are making the hammering sound while mining for gold and silver.

The goblins in this Viking tale are known for creating beautiful jewelry, a common theme throughout goblin folklore. Inside the cave, Freya sees a necklace. She is captivated by it and must have it at any cost. The goblins tell her they will give her the necklace if she gives each of them a sloppy kiss. Freya meets the goblins' demand, doling out the kisses. She then rushes back with the necklace to her husband Odur. He is disgusted when Freya tells him the story of how she acquired the beautiful necklace and runs from the palace. Days later, Freya goes to Odin and requests that she return the jewelry to the goblins, but Odin says she must wear it forever as a sign of her shame.

From the early days of the Vikings right through the twentieth century, Scandinavian nations have written much about goblins. Legendary Danish author Hans Christian Andersen featured goblins in his writings. The goblins in his fairy tale "The Elf Mound" are traders—a common depiction throughout goblin lore. However, Andersen also talks about his goblins as travelers, similar to later writers such as Tolkien. Andersen's goblins are also set in their ways. The Elf King in the tale has this to say about goblins: "They are thrifty travelers, they will come by ship when they have a chance.

The Viking goddess Freya is captivated by the beautiful jewelry created by these goblins.

I [the Elf King] wanted them to travel overland, by way of Sweden, but the old gentleman wouldn't hear of it. He [the goblin chief] doesn't keep up with the times, and I don't like that."

Norway is another nation rich in goblin lore. Members of the Viking Society for Northern Research noted in their 1898 annual journal: "And what country more suitable [than Norway] for the abode of elves, goblins and dwarfs than the deep-pine forests and birch groves which be scattered upon the rock-strewn uplands above the **fjord**." Author Beatrix Jungman stated that many Norwegian peasants in the early twentieth century talked about goblins with blue beards that haunted both the fields and fjords of the area. Some of these were considered good, and others bad. Either way, many folks blamed their luck on these goblins' deeds or misdeeds.

Especially since the nineteenth century, folklorists around the world have recorded stories about all kinds of goblins—from rather helpful household varieties such as Germany's *hausmänner* to much more **malevolent** ones like the spriggans that normally inhabit old castles and ruins in England. Scholar Patricia Monaghan believes that all goblins—from pookas to bogey—have their roots "in the Celtic version of the otherworld." Regardless of their origins, children and adults alike have been fascinated by tales of goblins.

A Mischievous Spirit in France

Many theories exist about the origin of the word "goblin." One of the most interesting involves a mischievous spirit that haunted the area around the town of Évreux in northwestern France. A twelfth-century English cleric named Ordericus Vitalis wrote about this spirit. According to legend, Saint Taurinus, the first bishop of Évreux, expelled this demon from the Temple of Diana in Évreux. Some say the demon took the forms of a lion, a bear, and a buffalo. In Old French this spirit was known as Gobelin, but in medieval Latin the spirit went by the name Gobelinus.

Common people of the area said that Saint Taurinus prevented this goblin from injuring them. He commanded the goblin to break its own **idols** or else be cast into a pit believed to lead to the underworld. Even though Gobelin was bound by Saint Taurinus to do no further injury to the inhabitants there, he continued to haunt the town in various forms. Choosing to lurk by the roadside or in out-of-the-way places, he delighted in mocking travelers and leading them astray. Yet after his dealings with the revered saint, Gobelin could no longer cause serious injury to people. The infamous goblin of Évreux merely annoyed people with harmless pranks instead.

This stained-glass window depicts a scene from Saint Taurinus's life.

3

DANCERS, CHANGELINGS, AND SHAPE-SHIFTERS

"The fact that no two descriptions seem to be the same attests to the shape-shifting abilities of this tricksy supernatural. A generally accepted image seems to be of a small human-shaped hairy being."

CAROL ROSE, *SPIRITS, FAIRIES, LEPRECHAUNS, AND GOBLINS: AN ENCYCLOPEDIA*

SINCE THE EARLIEST MYTHS, GOBLINS have possessed special powers. Given their fantastical status, perhaps it should not be surprising that goblins' talents run the gamut from dancing to jewelry-making to shape-shifting. Skills that might seem useless at first glance often turn out to be unique and powerful when wielded by goblin folk.

Around the globe, folktales describe goblins' excellent skills as miners. Sometimes goblins use this talent as a way to uncover silver or other precious materials for their own use. Perhaps there's a connection between goblins finding underground treasure and their talent as jewelry makers. After all, numerous legends describe goblins' talent with making jewelry. As seen in the last chapter's

Opposite: William Blake's watercolor illustration shows a goblin appearing to shape-shift. Goblins in folklore often change shape as a way to trick humans.

Viking folktale featuring Freya, goblin jewelry was sometimes used as a method of tempting not only humans but also deities.

The Dangers of Dancing

British and Scandinavian tales about goblins often mention these creatures dancing. Welsh poet Iolo Morganwg wrote about the ellylldans, describing how their slow dancing put a person to sleep. Another nineteenth-century story from Wales compared the wild, swift motion of goblin dancing to that of **Morris dancers**.

At first glance, dancing may seem harmless, or at least to be a relatively unimportant talent. Yet Norwegian goblin legends show that this skill can be used maliciously. Many old superstitions connected with Norwegian weddings involve the "hill people," another name for goblins, trolls, and similar creatures. Goblins were sometimes believed to have evil plans against weddings. Some legends feature goblins stealing brides and taking them to live underground with them. They did this so that humankind might not continue to grow in strength and numbers.

Even if the goblins did not break up a marriage, they did make mischief. The following anecdote depicts a terrible wedding misdeed:

> Over near Eidfjord [in western Norway], so the story goes, a bad spirit once took the form of a wandering fiddler and attended a wedding, offering to play for the evening dance, and he wielded his fiddle-bow with such magic power, that the bride danced and danced and could not stop, but danced until she died!

Shape-Shifting: More Goblin Trickery

In the preceding story, a goblin took the form of a human fiddler. Goblins' ability to shape-shift is essential to their mythology. Having the capability to change from one form to another is an extremely valuable power for goblins wanting to prank humans. This supernatural ability has captured the imaginations of storytellers for many centuries. The British goblins known as spriggans are normally very small but are said to be able to make themselves huge and terrifying like ginormous monsters. German kobolds are usually invisible but will sometimes materialize in the form of a person, an animal, or even an object. For example, a bad-tempered kobold might take the form of a feather and tickle the nose of a sleeping homeowner, making him sneeze.

A person dressed as a bugbear scares visitors at the Harbin International Ice and Snow Festival in China.

Another example of shape-shifting goblins are the bugbears of English lore. These malevolent spirits were believed to take the form of huge beasts or bears. They were thought to enjoy devouring badly behaved children and served as a way to threaten youngsters into acting well. People also called these goblins bugaboos.

Even Shakespeare's character Puck describes how he shape-shifts to lead people astray in *A Midsummer Night's Dream:*

I'll follow you, I'll lead you about a round,
Through bog, through bush, through brake, through **brier:**
Sometime a horse I'll be, sometime a hound,
A hog, a headless bear, sometime a fire

The Myth of the Changeling

A central form used in relation to goblins and shape-shifting is that of the changeling. One of goblins' favorite tricks is to kidnap a human baby from its crib and leave a changeling in its place. A changeling is actually a goblin baby and is far more troublesome than a normal human infant. The changeling typically looks just like the kidnapped human baby, though it may have some kind of giveaway feature—like pointed ears. American author John Greenleaf Whittier's nineteenth-century poem "The Changeling" told of these terrifying creatures:

Oh, fair and sweet was my baby,
Blue eyes, and hair of gold;
But this is ugly and wrinkled,
Cross, and cunning, and old.

The devil is trading a human baby back for a changeling in this fifteenth-century artwork.

Unlike human babies, changelings are mischievous like their fellow goblins. They also tend to have enormous appetites.

As you might imagine, when human parents discover the baby in their crib is actually a changeling, they are usually terrified. However, as told in numerous stories, it is possible to get a human baby back. The humans must trick a changeling into giving away its true goblin nature. One strategy is to pretend to brew water in the empty halves of an eggshell. This silly prank will fascinate the changeling, who is bound to talk, thus showing its true colors. Another idea is to pretend to throw the changeling into the hearth fire.

Once it has been discovered, a changeling has to escape—typically by flying up the chimney of the human home. Goblins will soon deliver the human baby back to his or her very relieved parents.

Other Abilities

In addition to being able to change shape, some goblins are also said to be expert imitators of sounds. A sixteenth-century writer refers to this ability in his writings: the day before a group of merchants comes to a country house in Italy, the people living there describe how they often hear what sounds like scales rattling, the ring of money, and even noises that seem like buying and selling are taking place. There are also other tales of goblins making sounds like those of rain or blowing wind on the night before a storm.

Brownies

A common and well-liked variety of goblin is the brownie, a creature that lives inside people's houses. This spirit is found throughout Scottish and English folklore. In southern England, this creature is known as Robin Goodfellow. Families believed their brownies brought good luck.

Brownies are commonly described as being brown, quite small, and like a shaggy person. They can wear tattered brown clothes or be naked. They may have noses or only two nostrils. Some legends show brownies' fingers as attached to each other via a web, like a duck's foot.

This illustration shows a brownie happily accepting a new cloak.

No matter how they look, brownies are perceived as being the most hardworking of the goblins. They do all kinds of dull and tiresome jobs—cleaning the barns or the house, plowing fields, grinding grain. In exchange for their labor, brownies were entitled to a bowl of cream and baked bread or cake. Any other kind of payment, such as new clothes, could be considered insulting to a brownie.

Criticism of a brownie's work was never well received. When a farmworker criticized how the brownie of Crenshaw Farm mowed and stacked the corn, the brownie had this to say:

> It's no weel mowed!
> Then it's ne'er to be mowed by me again;
> I'll scatter it owre the Raven Stane
> And they'll hae some wark ere it's mowed again.

This brownie then carried the corn 2 miles (3.2 kilometers) away to Raven Crag where he threw it into the river below. The brownie was never spied again at Cranshaw Farm.

4

THE PRINCESS AND THE GOBLIN

"They are always boring and blasting and breaking, you know."

GEORGE MACDONALD, *THE PRINCESS AND THE GOBLIN*

NE OF THE MOST WELL-KNOWN goblin myths is the children's fantasy *The Princess and the Goblin*, written by Scottish author George MacDonald in 1872. This book became one of the prime stories featuring goblins. During the nineteenth century, most frightening stories that were written and published for youngsters had two clear goals in mind. One was to teach them the morals of that time. The other was to show children that superstition, such as belief in goblins, was false and was perpetuated by wicked, foolish individuals.

The Princess and the Goblin was unique for the time because it portrayed young people behaving like children. Other stories during this time showed children behaving more like adults. The story's

Opposite:
This illustration from George MacDonald's book shows goblins living in underground caverns.

Miner boy Curdie follows his friend Princess Irene with his torch in a scene from *The Princess and the Goblin*.

main character, Princess Irene, does not always make good decisions. Like all children, there are bumps along her road to growing up. For example, Irene goes outside at night despite the danger of doing so. This idea of a rather imperfect young heroine was pretty revolutionary for its time. The story was also full of exciting, fantastic images and ideas that captivated young readers and were likely to inspire them to behave well.

The Goblins Underground

Set in a mountainous kingdom, the story takes place in and around the rural estate of eight-year-old Princess Irene. Irene's father is the king who rules over a large territory of valleys and mountains. Shortly after Irene's birth, her mother's health suffers and the princess is sent to live in a big country home on the side of a mountain. The young princess is taken care of by a nurse named Lootie. In many respects, Irene's mountain home is less important to the myth than what lies under it:

> These mountains were full of hollow places underneath; huge caverns, and winding ways … Now in these subterranean caverns lived a strange race of beings, called by some gnomes, by some kobolds, by some goblins. There was a legend current in the country that at one time they lived above ground and were very like other people.

The story suggests that at some point all of the goblins disappeared from the surface of the land. Some folks said that the king put too severe taxes on the goblins. Others said that he'd imposed stricter laws on them or had treated the goblins harshly. The legend went on to say that instead of moving to another country, these goblins all chose to take refuge in underground caverns. They only came out at night. MacDonald's goblins did not want to interact with "sun-people" (humans). So they kept busy when there was little chance of meeting

THE UNDERGROUND WORKERS

Tiny, muscular goblins wearing leather-type aprons work underground with axes.

up with either the miners below ground or the goat herders and other folks who lived in the vicinity. These goblins rarely showed themselves in any numbers, and never to many people at once. People who had caught a glimpse of the goblins said that over the generations, these creatures had changed form because they'd been living out of the sun in wet, dark, cold locations. As the goblins grew more misshapen and hideous, they became smarter as well. They delighted in annoying the people who lived in the open air above them.

The goblins in *The Princess and the Goblin* clung to their grudge against the king, his descendants, and other people who occupied the territory where they used to live. They took advantage of every opportunity to torment people. Their revenge techniques were often quite clever. At one point, the goblin king talks about trying

to starve Curdie, a miner boy who is a friend of Princess Irene but an enemy of the goblins:

> They [humans] are poor feeble creatures, those sun-people, and want to be always eating. *We* can go a week at a time without food, and be all the better for it; but I've been told *they* eat two or three times every day! Can you believe it? They must be quite hollow inside—not at all like us, nine-tenths of whose bulk is solid flesh and bone. Yes—I judge a week of starvation will do for him.

GOBLIN CHARACTERISTICS

Despite their small appearance, the goblins in MacDonald's tale are strong and crafty. They are also well organized, with their own king, queen, and government. One of the main conflicts in the story stems from the goblin king's plan to kidnap Princess Irene to marry his son Harelip. Thanks to some clever planning on the part of the human characters, this plan fails.

Much like earlier goblin tales, *The Princess and the Goblin* features goblins that are expert miners. MacDonald's story features the sounds of goblin pickaxes and hammers by night, just like in German kobold tradition, for example.

Some of the goblins' physical characteristics are played up in MacDonald's story. For example, they are said to have hard heads but very soft feet. During various encounters with the goblins, the character Curdie uses the weakness of goblin feet as a way to attack these enemies. While the goblin queen wears sturdy shoes made of granite, most of these creatures do not. Curdie stomps on many

goblins' feet, causing them to **recoil** from the miner boy. Even the goblin king howls pitifully when Curdie stomps on his feet.

Besides having weak feet, the goblins in *The Princess and the Goblin* are negatively impacted when they hear rhymes. Curdie thinks of rhymes as weapons when scheming for how to repel or harm his fantastical enemies.

Despite the death of many goblins in the story, *The Princess and the Goblin* has more of a "happily ever after" ending. This continues to be a common occurrence in fairy tales to this day. Not all of the goblins die at the end of MacDonald's book. In fact, there are some rather dramatic changes in the surviving creatures:

> A good many of the goblins with their creatures escaped from the **inundation** out upon the mountain. But most of them who remained grew milder in character, and indeed became very much like the Scotch Brownies. Their skulls became softer as well as their hearts, and their feet grew harder, and by degrees they became friendly with the inhabitants of the mountain and even with the miners.

Influence of the Story on Other Writers

Generations of writers have been influenced by *The Princess and the Goblin*. J. R. R. Tolkien is one example. He read MacDonald's stories as a child and also shared these goblin tales with his own children. Literary scholars point out that both MacDonald's and Tolkien's books feature an underground race of goblins. On a number of occasions, Tolkien referred to this similarity, hinting that his goblins in Middle Earth resembled those of George MacDonald. However, Tolkien's goblins also varied from the ones in MacDonald's tale for young readers. For one thing, Tolkien's goblins did not share the characteristic of soft feet. They also tended to be far more violent and destructive than the goblins portrayed in MacDonald's story.

C. S. Lewis, author of the Narnia series, was so impressed with MacDonald's tales that he referred to MacDonald as his "master." Lewis believed that MacDonald's works such as *The Princess and the Goblin* had a quality he sometimes called "holiness," other times "godliness." It may be important for readers to understand that both Lewis and MacDonald were devout Christians who aimed to incorporate morality and Christian values into their stories.

Another person who was greatly influenced by MacDonald's writing was G. K. Chesterton, author of *The Everlasting Man*. In particular, the sense of morality and mystical awareness that MacDonald was able to weave into books like *The Princess and the Goblin* resonated with Chesterton: "I for one can really testify to a book that has made a difference to my whole existence ... Of all the stories I have read, it remains the ... most like life. It is called *The Princess and the Goblin*."

Goblins on Halloween

In the past, some people believed that goblins and other monsters were able to wander about freely on Halloween. The holiday's origins date back to a pre-Christian Celtic festival called Samhain (SAH-wen). The Celts thought that November 1 marked the end of the harvest and the start of the New Year. They believed that the souls of the dead mixed and mingled among the living during this time. They also associated the fruits of the harvest with death and the supernatural.

Folks in Ireland had some particularly interesting ways to deal with these demons. Originally, people carved turnips or potatoes to look like hideous goblin faces. Then they placed either glowing coals or small candles inside. Townsfolk would put these carved root vegetables outside their homes and sometimes in their windows in order to frighten the actual goblins away. As waves of Irish immigrants came to live in America, this tradition was altered slightly. These new settlers discovered that pumpkins were abundant and pretty easy to carve, so they began carving them to scare away roaming goblins. Today, this holiday tradition remains an important part of Halloween festivities.

This poster advises people to not be afraid of goblins or ghosts.

Halloween Don'ts

Don't be scared of Goblins or Ghosts
Make a noise like an owl on Halloween
And the witches will come to drive them away
And they'll never come back for a year and a day

This little fat Goblin,
   A notable sinner,
Stole cabbages daily,
   For breakfast and dinner.

The Farmer looked sorry;
   He cried, and with pain,
"That rogue has been here
   For his cabbage again!"

That little plump Goblin,
   He laughed, "Ho! ho! ha!
Before me he catches,
   He'll have to run far."

That little fat Goblin,
   He never need sorrow;
He stole three to-day,
   And he'll steal more to-morrow.

5

TEMPTERS AND THIEVES

*"I have had some experience with goblins, and they are not nice creatures …
The goblins have no love for men, and not much for dragons."*

Piers Anthony, *Castle Roogna*

FROM THE EARLIEST FOLKLORE, PEOPLE have had somewhat of a love/hate relationship with goblins. Many folktales have portrayed goblins as enemies of humankind. Goblins commonly play the roles of tempter and thief. However, they can also show kindness. The ways in which goblins and humans interact has varied over the centuries and across different cultures. How people react to goblins depends on whether the storyteller depicts the mythical creatures as sinister, evil beings or as kindly, helpful ones.

TALENTED TEMPTERS

Throughout mythology, goblins have tempted people and even gods into bad behavior. For example, in Viking tales, the goddess Freya was tempted by the goblins' beautifully crafted jewelry. Her desire for what

Opposite: Kate Greenaway shows a cheeky, cabbage-stealing goblin in this illustration.

the goblins had led her to break the rules of proper social behavior. She was led down the dark path, so to speak, with dire consequences.

A tempting goblin from German folklore is Bruder Rausch, whose name roughly translates to "Brother **Intoxication**." According to legend, the devil sent the evil spirit Bruder Rausch to monasteries in the form of a monk. This goblin's role was to tempt monks into behaving badly, encouraging them to participate in activities like getting drunk. England had a very similar goblin called an abbey lubber. This goblin was reputed to dwell in British abbeys after the fifteenth century. Such tales of temptation by goblins typically reflect the perspective and religious values of their authors. Many Christian authors depicted demons as enemies of the soul. As a kind of demon, goblins too were enemies of Christianity.

Make no mistake, though. Goblins did not only tempt adults. Christina Rossetti was one of the best-known Christian poets of the nineteenth century. Her poem "Goblin Market" is an excellent example of how goblins were used to portray temptation and bad behavior. Much in the same way that Eve ate forbidden fruit in the Garden of Eden, Rossetti's goblins tempt young sisters Lizzie and Laura to buy and eat the fruit they are selling. When one sister refuses to eat their fruit, the goblins become enraged and attack her:

> Though the goblins cuffed and caught her ...
> Scratched her, pinched her black as ink,
> Kicked and knocked her,
> Mauled and mocked her,
> Lizzie uttered not a word

Not all humans are as able to resist fighting with nasty goblins as Rossetti's young character Lizzie. Curdie faces the goblins head-to-head in battle in George MacDonald's *The Princess and the Goblin*. Sometimes he succeeds in beating the evil creatures, while other times he is wounded.

Goblins as Thieves

In addition to the tempter, another common role of goblins in folkloric tales is that of the thief. Goblins tend to be small and quick. They often steal things in a very quiet manner, easily slipping away from the scene of the theft unnoticed. Sometimes goblins steal items, such as swords or knives, simply because they want these objects. In other instances, goblins steal items from people to use as ransom. Goblins are known to love treasure—gems, gold, and the like. These creatures may steal jewels or other valuable objects from their fellow goblins. This thieving behavior commonly leads to vicious conflicts between goblins.

Goblins also steal food throughout folklore. Despite their small stature, goblins are known for having huge appetites. They often put away far more food than an unsuspecting human could imagine. Nineteenth-century writer Kate Greenaway tells the tale of a mischievous goblin thief in her poem:

This little fat Goblin
A notable sinner,
Stole cabbages daily,
For breakfast and dinner.

Domestic Goblins

We know that not all folklore shows goblins in a bad light. Germany's kobolds often protect people from being wounded or killed in cave-ins in the mines. Some goblins, particularly house goblins or brownies, help people in daily life. These goblins sometimes do chores. In return, humans reward them with food and other comforts, like a warm place to live. German folklore features hausmänner (or "house men"), which are house fairies or elves of a domestic nature. Sometimes mischievous and other times useful, the hausmänner typically look for some type of material reward for their labor. Scottish author Andrew Lang's *Pink Fairy Book*, first published in 1897, contains a story called "The Browney at the Grocer's." The goblin in the story stays in the shop "because every Christmas Eve he'd get a bowl of porridge with a big lump of butter in it."

In England, stories about house goblins abound. These creatures have many names including hobgoblins, robgoblins, or even hobgoblinets. These spirits get their name from the word "hob" referring to the stove or hearth of a home. They love the warmth of stoves. They're attracted to these kitchen spaces since they cannot work with fire on their own. Some legends suggest that hobgoblins were originally more malicious but eventually settled in human residences to pester people.

While these goblins *could* choose to help at nearly any job if needed, they were known for their skill in certain tasks: threshing and grinding corn to make flour and churning milk to make butter. John Milton made reference both to these goblins' skills and rewards in his seventeenth-century poem "L'Allegro":

Tells how the **drudging** goblin sweat
To earn his cream-bowl duly set,
When in one night, ere glimpse of morn,
His shadowy **flail** hath thresh'd the corn

Bauchans or bogans are also English variations of hobgoblins. Considered to be nature spirits, these goblins tend to be relatively good-natured and helpful to humans. Often described as very ugly, bauchans will pull spiteful pranks, especially if they feel they have been offended in some way. People sometimes say that as constantly burning kitchen hearths have been replaced by electric and gas ranges, there has been a marked decline in the appearance of hobgoblins.

Protecting Against Goblins

Throughout history, people looked for ways to protect themselves against goblins. Since many European tales showed goblins to be enemies of Christianity, it seems fitting that religious articles were thought to protect humans against these creatures. Crosses and Bibles were among the items thought to keep goblins away. In some mining regions, people said specific prayers to protect themselves from being harmed by the tricks of the goblins. Salt and running water were also believed to repel goblins. It's interesting to note that many of these same objects were used against other mythical creatures such as vampires.

Hanging an iron horseshoe on the front door was thought to keep goblins from entering one's home.

Since all fairies don't like iron, some folks believed that hanging an iron horseshoe over their front door would prevent goblins from coming into their home. If someone had to go out at night on his own, he could protect himself from goblin tricks by wearing his clothes inside out. Another protective strategy was to tie a piece of red thread to one's clothes.

Of course, some people avoided goblins' pranks by staying in their favor, leaving out milk and bread for the goblins to munch on at night. Also, since goblins like to trick and punish bad people, if a person behaved well, it was thought the goblins might be less likely to harm him or her.

6

ASIAN GOBLIN MYTHS

"He [the tengu] appeared as a demon of the woods and mountain recesses, who deceived mankind."

M. W. De Visser, *Transactions of the Asiatic Society of Japan, Volumes 35–36*

WHILE MANY GOBLIN TALES TAKE place in Europe, fables about these creatures also exist in other parts of the world. Two Asian nations rich in goblin mythology are Korea and Japan. Both countries have captivating and varied goblin tales. Much like Christianity played a role in Europe's goblin mythology, traditional folk religions influenced Asian goblin tales.

KOREAN GOBLIN LORE

Since before 1000 BCE, shamanism has been a part of the belief system on the Korean Peninsula. Shamanism involves the worship of spirits that are believed to inhabit all objects on Earth—from plants and trees to animals and insects. Goblins are thought to be the spirits of wicked people who have been trapped in **purgatory**. Unfortunately,

Opposite: Korea has a rich goblin mythology tradition. There, one can find artwork featuring scary goblins like this one.

these spirits, including goblins, must wander the world, leaving behind them a wake of hardship for people.

Korean goblins, known as *doggabi* or *dokkaebi*, play an important role in the nation's folktales. These goblins often come out at night and love making mischief. Dokkaebi usually reward good people and punish the bad folks. They play nasty tricks on bad people. They also enjoy playing games. Dokkaebi sometimes challenge wayward travelers to a Korean wrestling match, known as a *ssireum*. If the challenged individual wins the match, he gains the right to pass the goblin. Some dokkaebi tales suggest that anyone trying to beat a dokkaebi cannot win by pushing it from the left-hand side, only from the right. Other folklore say the challenged individual just has to push the dokkaebi to win, since the Korean goblin has only one leg.

Like most goblins, dokkaebi commonly have frightening appearances, but other times they look rather cute, tall, and skinny—quite different from many other goblins. These Korean goblins have magic mallets. In some tales, these mallets have the ability to turn everything into gold. Goblin mallets can also change people's fortunes. In Kathleen Seros's account of the Korean folktale "The Magic Mallet," goblins use the magic mallet to make a boy's tongue 100 feet (30.5 m) long as a punishment for his greedy behavior.

Even today, dokkaebi are remembered in some Korean cultural celebrations. An example is a ceremony called Yeonggam Nori (*yeonggam* is another Korean word for goblin and is also a god). This rite is held on Jeju, a volcanic island that lies southwest of the Korean Peninsula. This ceremony is focused on exorcising, or expelling, goblins from the island. It is also seen as a healing ritual. To prepare for this ceremony, people build a small straw raft that they place next to an altar. Two apprentice shamans wear yeonggam masks and costumes. Depending

on how formal the ritual is, these masks can be made from rice paper or thicker, painted, cardboard-like paper.

During the Yeonggam Nori rite, each costumed shaman holds a torch in one hand and a "pipe" made from a stick stuck into an apple in the other hand. The ceremony features a play, where the dressed-up shamans recite theatrical dialogue and act out roles. Within the realm of Korean mythology, Yeonggam is a god of fishing, seafaring, and wealth. This deity also acts as a village guardian and features some characteristics of a blacksmith. People say that Yeonggam sometimes wishes illness on people. The Yeonggam Nori rite is considered so important to Korea's national heritage that it was designated as an **Intangible** Cultural Treasure in 1971.

Japanese Goblin Mythology

Much like Korea, Japan also has a strong goblin folklore tradition. Japanese goblins are known as *tengu*. They have been part of Japan's rich mythology for many centuries. Scholars debate about the exact origin of the tengu. Numerous researchers believe that Japan's tengu stem from Chinese folkloric creatures called *t'ien-kou* ("celestial dog"). These Chinese forest demons are believed to have come to Japan in the sixth and seventh centuries CE.

In Japanese legend, it's common for tengu to live in the mountains. They can take different forms. Some appear as old men who have long noses and commonly walk barefoot. These long-nosed goblins are known as *konoha tengu*. They are often associated with good harvests. Today there are festivals in cities around Japan that celebrate the tengu. For example, Shimokita Tengu Matsuri is held in Tokyo each year. It features a tengu parade and traditional drumming. People attending this festival can participate in a bean-throwing ceremony where they

At a shrine festival in Tokyo, Japan, a man wears a goblin mask.

throw beans at people in demon costumes to ensure good fortune and health for the upcoming year.

Karasu tengu look more like crows (*karasu* means "crow" in Japanese). They feature the beak, claws, and wings of a bird while also having the body of a man. This bird-human variety of tengu has caused other scholars to suggest that the tengu are a variation of Buddhist guardian deities called *garuda*. Like tengu, the garuda had human bodies but their heads and wings were those of a bird. Both tengu and garuda can take different forms. Just like in some European legends, tengu were sometimes described as shape-shifters; these goblins could turn themselves into human form and mislead people.

In earlier tales about tengu, these goblins performed wicked acts such as kidnapping and eating human children or starting fires. However, the tengu were also known for their skills as warriors and for their swordsmanship. Japanese folklore has made a connection between these goblins and the martial arts tradition This link dates back as far as about the tenth century CE, though it became clearer during the fourteenth century as the culture of *ryu*, or formal martial arts schools, became established.

The history of tengu has been linked over the centuries with that of *yamabushi*, or mountain priests. In fact, some people believed that many of the yamabushi were actually tengu trying to wreak havoc on local villagers. Yet despite this tengu-priest connection, it has been common for tengu to be portrayed as enemies of Buddhism. Tales often show the tengu kidnapping priests, even going so far as to leave these spiritual leaders tied to the tops of trees. The tengu would use their powers to put hateful, greedy, or proud ideas into the minds of the priests they'd captured.

In a rather strange shift, the character of tengu started to change as the thirteenth century came to a close. While the tengu had up to this point been almost exclusively characterized as evil creatures, some later legends depicted tengu as good-natured. Some of these Japanese goblins even worked to help people. It may seem bizarre, but these kinder, more respectable tengu were portrayed as protectors of some Buddhist temples, particularly those in the mountains.

MINAMOTO YOSHITSUNE AND TENGU

One of the most popular Japanese historical figures of the twelfth century is Minamoto Yoshitsune. For hundreds of years, this famous warrior's daring exploits have captured the imaginations of many Japanese writers, playwrights, and other artists. Yoshitsune is also celebrated for his connection to the tengu.

As an infant, Yoshitsune's father, Minamoto Yoshitomo, was defeated during the Heiji Distrubance of 1159. Rather than killing Minamoto's child, conqueror Taira Kiyomori sent little Yoshitsune to live in a monastery near the capital of Kyoto. Here Yoshitsune trained to become a Buddhist priest. Living high in the mountains, the young Yoshitsune got tired of life in the monastery. Eventually, he uncovered the truth about his heritage and became keen on seeking revenge for his father's defeat. By night, Yoshitsune liked to sneak out, training himself with a wooden sword he'd made.

According to legend, a tengu who lived in the forests near the monastery discovered Yoshitsune. A tengu leader named Sojobo offered to teach Yoshitsune his warfare secrets, particularly his techniques for swordsmanship. Sojobo did this because he knew that Yoshitsune would start up trouble and bring death to many enemies. After his intensive study with Sojobo, Yoshitsune became an excellent warrior. He eventually left the mountain monastery, gathered and organized forces, and defeated the Taira clan in 1185 at the Battle of Dannoura.

GREMLINS AND GOBLIN GAMES

"They're goblins, Harry. Clever as they come, goblins, but not the most friendly of beasts."

J. K. ROWLING, *HARRY POTTER AND THE SORCERER'S STONE*

I T COULD BE SAID THAT THE NINETEENTH century was the **heyday** for goblins, at least from a literary perspective. Poems and stories about these mythical creatures abounded during that time in locations from Europe to Asia. Some authors clearly used the antics of goblins as ways to scare people into behaving well. However, as the nineteenth century drew to a close, many people expressed their disbelief, or at least seriously questioned the belief, in goblins. In his essay "God In Human Thought," Henry A. Nelson had this to say about the societal changes in perceptions of goblins:

Opposite:
A scene from the 1990 film *Gremlins 2: The New Batch.*

What is it which has rid our minds of the belief in goblins and in witches, which possessed many intelligent and candid minds of former generations? It is simply this: that we have found more reasonable ways of accounting for all the phenomena which used to be regarded as proofs of their existence. Physical science has emancipated us from such superstition.

The Evolving Goblin

Did everyone stop believing in and writing about goblins as we entered the twentieth and twenty-first centuries? Of course not. Even today, people around the globe continue to believe in and tell tales about goblins. However, more modern writers and artists have sometimes changed the appearances and qualities of goblins in their works. For example, author J. R. R. Tolkien brought goblinkind into a more evil realm. Tolkien's book *The Hobbit* features flocks of tunnel-dwelling goblins as evil, violent opponents who battle men, dwarves, elves, and other fantastical creatures.

A new variety of goblin that captured people's imaginations is the gremlin. They first appeared during World War I, though their popularity really took off from World War II on. Gremlins represent a new variation on goblinkind because they fit in with the more modern, technologically advanced era. They are excellent at working with tools and complicated machinery. According to legend, gremlins once aided people in the development of new inventions. However, humans did not give credit to their goblin assistants. To get back at the greedy people, gremlins made their machines break down.

Gremlins can be blamed for many little mishaps that happen in a household. Did the car not start on a cold day? Did your alarm clock not go off in the morning, making you late for school? Did your bagel burn in the toaster? These are all the types of nuisances with which gremlins might annoy you. The 1984 film *Gremlins* was hugely popular with people of all ages. In this movie, the tiny American town of Kingston Falls is thrown into chaos when a bank teller mistakenly releases these creatures after he gets one as a new pet. In the film, the rules for how to avoid trouble with a goblin are as follows: "Don't expose him to bright light. Don't ever get him wet. And don't ever, ever feed him after midnight." After this advice is ignored, the gremlins cause all kinds of trouble. They steal cookies, make a colossal mess of someone's kitchen, and wreak havoc all over town.

Celebrated British author J. K. Rowling certainly kept goblins in the limelight in her Harry Potter series. Just as earlier mythology depicted goblins' interest in treasure, Rowling's Harry Potter books also show this connection. Throughout the series, goblins are in

Many goblins in the Harry Potter books are pale, with pointy noses and ears. This one works at Gringotts Bank.

charge of protecting gems, gold, and other valuables at Gringotts, the bank of the wizarding world. In terms of appearance, Rowling's goblins typically are short, have fair skin, pointed noses, rather dome-shaped heads, and very long feet and fingers.

GOBLINS AND GAMES

In addition to literature and film, another way in which goblins have flourished in popular culture is through the world of games. An extremely popular game featuring goblins is Dungeons & Dragons (D&D). In this role-playing game, goblins follow in the lore that portrays them as malicious and evil. Their skin can range from yellow to orange or red, and they often wear dark leather garments. Some folks compare the goblins of D&D to German kobolds. The game also features hobgoblins.

Other modern-day games featuring goblins include Warhammer and Magic: The Gathering. The frightening-looking playing pieces of the board game Warhammer depict goblins with green skin. Their goal is to fight anything in their way, following the combative

A group of people evaluate their cards while playing Magic: The Gathering.

goblin tendencies seen in Tolkien's works. The card game Magic: The Gathering has many folkloric characters, such as a Goblin King. The game's Goblin Sharpshooter is known for his skill in wiping out elves. Some goblins in this card game are helpful, while others are more vicious.

Other Goblin Mythology

We know that goblins persist in current games, literature, and movies to this day. While modern-day storytellers tend to write epic sagas of goblins more infrequently, not everyone has given up on belief in these and other fantastical creatures. One country where such supernatural beliefs remain quite strong is Iceland. While the word *alfar*, meaning "elf," first appeared here in Viking-era poems that date back to about 1000 CE, the elf tradition lives on today. Some scholars have commented on how the geography and history of the country create an almost perfect setting for magical creatures. These "hidden people" are known in Icelandic as *huldufolk*.

It's not just a few random people who believe in supernatural beings here. In a 1998 survey, 54.4 percent of Icelanders said that they believed elves (another type of fantasy creature) exist. As supernatural seer and political activist Ragnhildur Jónsdóttir recently said, "If this was just one crazy lady talking about invisible friends, it's really easy to laugh about that ... But to have people through hundreds of years talking about the same things, it's beyond one or two crazy ladies. It is part of the nation."

In 2010, a former member of the Icelandic parliament named Árni Johnsen flipped his SUV on an icy road, **careened** off a cliff,

This Japanese manuscript from around 1600 CE shows armed goblins wielding various weapons.

and survived without serious injury. Johnsen credited his survival to elves living in a boulder near the site of the car wreck. In 2013, protestors who call themselves Friends of the Lava fought against a proposed road-building project. Some feared that the road would displace certain supernatural forces that live within the volcanic rubble of the area and worried that these beings might cause trouble if the road were built.

Several alternative media outlets in Africa also noted goblin-related troubles in 2014. These stories reported goblins as making successful businessmen poor, burning houses down, and even poisoning people's food. After the death of her sister, a South African woman had this to say: "All the food that comes into my yard is being poisoned by an invisible thing. I think it's a *tokoloshe* [cross between a gremlin and a zombie] and it wants to kill my whole family." Another story from Zimbabwe reported that a school shut down because goblins were attacking teachers. Belief in the supernatural continues to be widespread in this southern African nation.

However detailed goblin folklore might be, questions remain. Does anyone still believe in goblins? Can we be sure they don't exist? Perhaps Henry Nelson's open-minded approach leaves room for people to make up their own minds:

> Some have grown up in the belief of goblins and witches, and in their educated maturity have found valid reasons for abandoning such belief as sheer superstition. But ... there is a liability to become **morbidly** distrustful to all that was early learned, of all the old beliefs ... We ought not relinquish them until we have fairly and fully considered the evidence on which they rest, and have found it insufficient to support them.

Throughout history, goblins have been a part of folklore as well as real-life encounters. Perhaps their true forms will never be fully realized, but societies around the world will continue to speculate and celebrate them as fantastical creatures.

GLOSSARY

abound To be present in great quantities.

Bohemian Describing a region of Europe consisting largely of the present-day western Czech Republic, known for its rich art and literary scene in the nineteenth and twentieth centuries.

brier A mass of prickly or thorny bushes.

captivating Attracting or holding the interest of someone.

careen To move swiftly in an uncontrolled way.

Celtic A term used to describe a group of peoples who lived mostly in what is now Ireland, Scotland, and Wales during pre-Roman times.

countenance Face or appearance.

drudging Doing dull or hard work.

fjord A narrow inlet of the sea located between cliffs.

flail A tool used to thresh grain by hand.

heyday The time of greatest popularity or strength.

idol A statue or object sometimes worshipped by people.

intangible Impossible to touch.

intoxication The condition of being drunk.

inundation A flood.

labyrinth A maze or place full of passageways that make it hard to get around.

malevolent Spiteful; showing ill will.

morbid Characterized by having sick or gloomy ideas and feelings.

Morris dancers People who perform a type of lively English dance, often outdoors.

pagan A person who holds religious beliefs that are outside of the world's main religions.

purgatory A place where the souls of sinners are punished after death before going to heaven.

ratel A kind of badger.

recoil To retreat or shrink back.

stile A step or set of steps for passing over a wall or fence.

To Learn More About Goblins

Books

Berk, Ari. *The Secret History of Hobgoblins*. Somerville, MA: Candlewick Press, 2012.

Currie, Stephen. *Goblins*. Monsters and Mythical Creatures. San Diego, CA: ReferencePoint Press, 2010.

Sautter, A. J. *A Field Guide to Goblins, Gremlins, and Other Wicked Creatures*. Fantasy Field Guides. North Mankato, MN: Capstone Press, 2014.

Website

Monstrous.com: Goblins

faerie.monstrous.com/goblins.htm

This website gives detailed information about goblins, including what they look like and the tricks they like to play on humans.

Video

The Princess and the Goblin. Directed by József Gémes. Siriol Productions, 1991. DVD.

Bibliography

Andersen, Hans Christian. "The Elf Mound." The Hans Christian Andersen Center. Retrieved April 2, 2015. http://www.andersen.sdu.dk/vaerk/hersholt/TheElfMound_e.html.

BBC. "Viking Sagas." BBC Learning School Radio. Retrieved April 10, 2015. www.bbc.co.uk/schoolradio/subjects/english/viking_sagas.

Briggs, Katharine. *An Encyclopedia of Fairies: Hobgoblins, Brownies, Bogies, And Other Supernatural Creatures*. New York: Pantheon Books, 1976.

Jacobs, Ryan. "Why So Many Icelanders Still Believe in Invisible Elves." *The Atlantic*, October 29, 2013. Retrieved May 7, 2015. http://www.theatlantic.com/international/archive/2013/10/why-so-many-icelanders-still-believe-in-invisible-elves/280783.

Lang, Andrew. *Pink Fairy Book*. New York: The Viking Press, 1982.

Leland, Charles Godfrey. *Etruscan Roman Remains in Popular Tradition*. London, UK: T. Fisher Unwin, 1892.

Lindsey, John. "Japan's Mythical Martial Arts Masters: Did Winged Goblins Teach the Ninja and the Samurai?" *Black Belt Magazine*, March 1989, 56–59.

MacDonald. George. *The Princess and the Goblin*. Philadelphia: David McKay Company, 1920.

Melville, Francis. *The Book Of Faeries: A Guide to the World of Elves, Pixies, Goblins, and Other Magic Spirits*. Hauppauge, NY: Barron's, 2002.

Mills, Claudia, ed. *Ethics and Children's Literature*. Farnham, UK: Ashgate Publishing, Ltd., 2014.

Milton, John. "L'Allegro." Poetry Foundation. Retrieved April 13, 2015. http://www.poetryfoundation.org/poem/173997.

Monaghan, Patricia. *The Encyclopedia of Celtic Mythology and Folklore*. New York: Infobase Publishing, 2009.

Myung-sub, Chung, ed. *Encyclopedia of Korean Folk Literature*. Seoul, South Korea: National Folk Museum of Korea, 2014.

Nelson, Henry A. "God In Human Thought." *Dickinson's Theological Quarterly 2* (1876).

Robinson, Martin. *Seoul*. Oakland, CA: Lonely Planet, 2006.

Rose, Carol. *Spirits, Fairies, Leprechauns, and Goblins: An Encyclopedia*. New York: W. W. Norton & Company, 1996.

Rossetti, Christina. *Goblin Market*. New York: Stonehill Publishing Company, 1975.

Sikes, Wirt. *British Goblins: Welsh Folk-Lore, Fairy Mythology, Legends And Traditions*. Boston, MA: James R. Osgood and Company, 1881.

Viking Society for Northern Research. "Saga-Book." Retrieved April 10, 2015. www.vsnr.org/saga-book.

Vitalis, Ordericus. *The Ecclesiastical History of England and Normandy*. London, UK: Henry G. Bohn, 1854.

Whittier, John Greenleaf. Complete Poetical Works. Boston: J.R. Osgood and Company, 1876.

Index

Page numbers in **boldface** are illustrations. Entries in **boldface** are glossary terms.

About the Author

Alicia Z. Klepeis loves to research fun and out-of-the-ordinary topics that make nonfiction exciting for readers. Alicia began her career at the National Geographic Society. She is the author of several nonfiction kids' books, including *Africa*, *The World's Strangest Foods*, *Understanding Saudi Arabia Today*, *Bizarre Things We've Called Medicine*, and *Vampires: The Truth Behind History's Creepiest Bloodsuckers*. Her fictional titles include the picture book *Francisco's Kites*, as well as a series of world adventures chapter books. She has also written over one hundred articles in magazines such as *National Geographic Kids*, *Kiki*, and *FACES*. Alicia is currently working on a middle-grade novel as well as several projects involving international food, American history, and world cultures. She lives with her family in upstate New York.